IMAGES OF
CANTERBURY

IMAGES OF CANTERBURY

Publishing coordination:
Media House Europe
Sittingbourne, Kent.

**Kent Messenger
Group Newspapers**

The Breedon Books
Publishing Company
Derby

First published in Great Britain by
The Breedon Books Publishing Company Limited
44 Friar Gate, Derby, DE1 1DA.
1997

ISBN 1 85983 097 8

Printed and bound by Butler & Tanner, Frome, Somerset.
Jacket printed by Lawrence Allen Ltd, Weston-super-Mare, Somerset.
Colour film by RPS Ltd of Leicester.

Contents

Introduction 6

Around the Walls of the City 8

City Life 23

Flooding, Fires and Bad Weather 37

Country Matters 46

Church, MPs and Royalty 52

Canterbury at War 62

Famous Faces 92

Farewell to the Old 103

Sports, Leisure, Recreation 113

Inside the Walls 129

Civic and Ceremonial 148

Hello to the New 159

Protest 170

Army Life 175

From the Air 178

Outside the Walls 185

Subscribers 192

Introduction

NINETY minutes was all it took to change the face of Canterbury for ever. In one terrifying raid in the early hours of 1 June 1942, a large part of the city centre was destroyed or badly damaged.

As planners began to outline their vision for post-war development, the rows began — and sometimes it seems as though they have never stopped. The people with the power to change the city's future stepped away from the bombs and into a minefield.

We must be grateful that the more fanciful plans never came to pass. Some schemes, for example, envisaged new roads cutting a swathe through the city centre to improve traffic flows; and if that meant the demolition of sound (and attractive) buildings, so be it. Such was the scope of early blueprints that some guardians of our past feared they would achieve what Hitler had failed to finish; the destruction not just of part of our history but of the city's character, too.

But the planners believed they had logic on their side. Perhaps the most robust explanation of their actions was given by John Boyle, Town Clerk for 30 years from 1942-72, who often voiced his belief that what was done was done for the best — or, at least, with the best of motives. And the city fathers did, indeed, try to be visionary: planning for the growth in traffic they knew would come; accommodating a bigger bus station and a multi-storey car park within the city walls for everyone's convenience; knocking down 'slums' to build brighter, warmer homes; improving, in their view, that which needed improving.

Their beliefs seemed to fit in with the spirit of the age. Out with the old; in with the new. A unique chance to sweep away the worst of centuries past and build a brave new Elizabethan world. And, in truth, not every building that survived the war — intact or barely damaged — was worth saving. Some were dark and grim (at best nondescript), industrial or commercial, whose passing was not much mourned.

Yet sometimes it is easy to look back and regret — regret the loss of grand St George's Terrace, perched above the city wall; the broad, tree-filled moat before the ring road ate into it; the junction that was Wincheap Green before it became a roundabout; the shops and cattle market in the St George's area; the little lost lanes; and the old Longmarket.

But where do you stop? We curse the car while using it; and bemoan the loss of small shops while stocking up at the supermarket. So, perhaps because of the big changes, we now make greater efforts to accommodate the past elsewhere. Where once we demolished, we renovate; where once we condemned, we rebuild.

Conservation is the current philosophy — but it, too, has its detractors. Its legacy, say some, is pastiche at the expense of innovation. The post-war development of the Longmarket has already fallen victim to this change in style: an improvement or a lost opportunity to show future generations what the 1990s could offer in good design?

Of course, Canterbury has also changed in many other ways — each change influencing development elsewhere. Two decades after the war ended the University of Kent opened; so, too, did the new Technical College and Christ Church College. They brought thousands of new people, staff and students, to the city — many with new ideas and new needs. And as standards of living rose, and more people bought cars and more roads were built to make it easier for them to travel, then travel they did — as shoppers from East Kent attracted to our stores; as pilgrims drawn by the Cathedral; or as visitors on a well-beaten trail to our historic landmarks.

Once the High Street was (incredible though it now seems) the main A2 route between London and the coast; and some of the pictures in this book testify to its busy pavements, filled with pedestrians anxious to avoid stepping into the path of passing lorries and double-decker buses. Now that same artery is traffic-free but all too often clogged with thousands of people, milling slowly past shops whose individuality has been lost to chains.

Some people who live here now — particularly those whose memories are of a quieter, less bustling city — feel that the needs of residents are sometimes ignored in preference to the needs of those just passing through. Perhaps what some feel most is the perceived loss of community spirit — the sense of being, in some ways, a neighbour to everyone encountered in the city.

Canterbury, though, is still often described as a big village, where social circles overlap and interlock. Conversations with city strangers often reveal them to be friends of friends of friends. So how much more true this must have been when the city was smaller and more self-contained; when Cricket Week and the carnival were calendar highlights; when a meander down the High Street also meant the chance to catch up on gossip.

In those days (and how long ago a quarter of a century can sometimes seem) Canterbury was a county borough, giving the city not only a status which seemed to reflect its importance in the history of this country but also giving it more control over its spending and more power in its decisions. And regional importance was also reflected in the existence of The Buffs, the regiment that was home to East Kent soldiery. But the writing was on the wall. The Buffs disappeared, swallowed up, eventually, by the new, greater regional Queen's Regiment; and so, too, was Canterbury to lose its county borough status in 1974, becoming merely another district council in the county that surrounded it.

This book aims to give a taste of life in Canterbury during those years, particularly in the war and the 25 years after that. It is not a comprehensive history but it will illustrate some of the things we have lost — and some we have gained. But do the images here seem to illustrate a city that was once more certain of its sense of community and its place in the world? Or do they show how much more vibrant Canterbury became as the decades passed?

Views will vary, of course. What is certain, however, is that the city faces more big changes in the years ahead, particularly with the redevelopment of the Whitefriars area and the growing demands of tourism. How those changes are tackled may depend on what has been learned from the past pictured in these pages.

But that story is one for the next Millennium.

Around the City Wall

1935 July: The Tower House in the Westgate Gardens had two additional gabled portions until they were demolished in 1937, after the house was given to the city by Stephen and Catherine Williamson (who became the first woman mayor of the city in 1938). The building has been the Mayor's Parlour since 1962.

1952 May: The Westgate and (right) Holy Cross Church, which was later to become the new Guildhall.

1968 May: The old cattle market site outside the city wall was used latterly for car parking. This unusual view through a bastion on the city wall looks towards the old crossroads at St George's Gate. All was to change when the roundabout was built as part of the ring road.

1968 October: Canterbury newsagent and tobacconist Eric Pettit moved from St George's Gate, where the family business had been for 118 years, to Burgate to make way for the second stage of the ring road. Here, the building stands alone as modern Canterbury rises up behind it.

1958: The old Co-op in Lower Bridge Street at St George's Gate. The building next to it was destroyed in the war. This area changed dramatically when the second stage of the ring road was built in the 1960s.

1965 October: Looking towards St George's Place before the second stage of the ring road consigned most of these buildings to history. The photographer was standing near St George's Clocktower. The tree was by the old cattle market site.

1938 March: St George's Terrace rises above the cattle market, which used to be outside the city wall near what is now St George's roundabout. The new cattle market at St Stephen's opened in 1955.

1946 November: The old crossroads at St George's Gate from Upper Bridge Street. Many of the buildings disappeared to make way for St George's roundabout and the ring road.

1952 November: Post-war Canterbury takes shape in the St George's area. Riceman's has yet to be built; and Pettit and Son tobacconists still occupies its site at St George's Gate.

1956 January: Workmen begin to remove the trees at the old cattle market site outside the city wall in Upper Bridge Street, opposite the Flying Horse.

1969 September: The old crossroads at St George's Gate can just be made out to the right of the ABC Cinema. But, as this view from the roof of the *Kentish Gazette* office in St George's Place shows, dramatic changes were underway.

1969 October: As the second stage of the ring road progresses, the 'massive roundabout at St George's Gate' was brought into use for the first time. Traffic lights were removed by the pedestrian subway, which was still being completed.

1949: Looking down Lower Bridge Street towards its junction with Burgate. These buildings (left) were demolished in 1969 to make way for the ring road, revealing a stretch of the city wall.

1952 Autumn: The Royal East Kent Yeomanry Memorial was moved from its site by the old cattle market, where it had stood since 1922, to a new position on the site of St Mary Bredman's Church in the High Street (by Nason's).

A view of Riding Gate roundabout showing the Victorian pedestrian bridge, which was moved in 1970, the Invicta engine, which stood on the site from 1906-69, and a collapsed section of city wall.

Looking along Pin Hill towards Riding Gate. The broad, tree-filled moat was lost to the ring road widening in the late 1960s.

1955 September: The Invicta engine at the Riding Gate as work begins on the new roundabout. The trees behind are on the site of what is now the fire station, formerly occupied by a blitzed house called The Limes.

1953 February: The Invicta locomotive outside the city walls at Riding Gate. It was built by Robert Stephenson and Co for the Canterbury and Whitstable Railway but was not powerful enough and was soon replaced. It was donated to the city in 1906 and had stood at this site since then. In February 1968 it was moved to Dane John Gardens to make way for the ring road. It was taken to the National Railway Museum for restoration in 1977 and is now on display at the Heritage Museum in Canterbury.

1952 November: Before the second stage of the ring road in the late 1960s the moat at Pin Hill seemed almost rural.

1969 March: The road at Pin Hill during work on the second stage of the ring road. Note the terrace (right) which was opposite Canterbury East station until it was demolished in the 1980s.

1952 November: A crazy paving path winds through the moat at Pin Hill in the shadow of Dane John. This idyllic scene fell victim to the ring road. Peacocks once strutted there in the 1930s — bringing complaints about noise from those who lived nearby.

1955 November: Looking across the Riding Gate roundabout from Upper Bridge Street towards the site of the police station, which opened a decade later.

Looking down Watling Street past the Riding Gate Inn, which was damaged during the war and demolished in 1955 to make way for the Riding Gate roundabout.

1961 Autumn: This view of Wincheap Green looks along Pin Hill from where Wincheap roundabout is today. The Castle Hotel (left) was pulled down in 1963 and most of the buildings from left to centre were demolished to make way for the ring road within a few years. St Andrew's Presbyterian Church was pulled down in 1973. The Man of Kent (building with white top, centre) was then at the junction of Pin Hill and Castle Row. The right hand half of the building was demolished to make way for the ring road while the left hand side became a private home. The name Man of Kent transferred to the former Station Hotel at Wincheap roundabout.

1961 April: Wincheap Grove was a cul-de-sac which led from Castle Street down towards St Mildred's Church. It was demolished this year to make way for the ring road. This was the view up towards Castle Street.

1961 Autumn: Wincheap Grove after demolition, looking away from Castle Street across open land roughly along the line of the Rheims Way that was to replace it.

1961 May: This unusual view looks from the moat at Pin Hill towards the back of St Andrew's Presbyterian Church at Wincheap Green. The houses (left to centre) were opposite Canterbury East station and were demolished in the 1980s.

1961 May: Before the roundabout was built, Wincheap and Castle Street were, in effect, one continuous road — with the Castle taking its place in a row of buildings. But the buildings here — a large house called The Cedars, used latterly by British Road Services, and the homes around Wincheap Grove — were pulled down to make way for the Rheims Way.

1961 May: Looking down Pin Hill towards Wincheap Green from Castle Row. All the buildings from right to centre were demolished because of the ring road.

1968 May: Unrecognisable today, a view down Lower Bridge Street towards what is now St George's roundabout. The Saracen's Head pub (right), on the corner of Burgate, was demolished in 1969 to make way for the ring road.

City Life

1961 August: Concern for animal rights means this is a sight that is unlikely ever to be seen again. Elephants from Sir Robert Fossett's circus make their way down Broad Street to Beverley Fields.

1952 September: Members and officers of the city council, led by the Mayor, Councillor John Barrett, visited the old Canterbury fire station in Old Dover Road and watched a rescue demonstration. The old fire station and divisional headquarters used to be between St Lawrence Close and St Lawrence Road until the new fire station opened at Riding Gate roundabout in 1967.

1953 September: Signalman Arthur Miles, 35, back in Barham after more than two years in a North Korean prison camp, with his daughter Gladys, six, and her dog, Suzy. He had been taken prisoner at the Battle of Imjin River while serving with the Royal Corps of Signals.

1955 September: A boy is 'bumped' during a Beating the City Bounds ceremony, watched by pupils from the Girls' Technical School. About 60 people took part. Boundary stones were bumped, the *Kentish Gazette* reported, to ensure that they were firmly fixed — and to help those being bumped to remember where they were.

1955 December: Hundreds of people joined in carol singing round the illuminated Christmas tree in the Marlowe Theatre car park on Christmas Eve, when the Archbishop, Dr Geoffrey Fisher, gave the Blessing.

1965: Students from Christ Church College line up after a hectic 60-yard pancake race from Burgate to the Longmarket. Their race was held on the Saturday before Shrove Tuesday because they had teaching practise on the day itself.

1955 April: Kent Scouts parade at Longport coach park ready for the final dismissal after their St George's Day procession to the Cathedral. Note the old Kent and Canterbury Hospital building, which closed as a hospital in 1937 and was subsequently used as the Canterbury Technical College and Technical School for Boys. It was demolished in 1977.

1965 May: A vain attempt is made to empty the River Stour with buckets at the King's Bridge during rag week, when students from Christ Church College, Wye and Nonington Colleges took part in stunts around the city.

1953 November: Harry Amess, corporation car park attendant, arrived at work 10 minutes early for four years to feed over 50 sparrows, a blackbird and few Cathedral pigeons every morning at his wooden hut at Broad Street car park.

1968 May: Members of the King's School Madrigal Society ascended the Bell Harry Tower of the Cathedral every year at 7am to sing on Ascension Day.

1970 April: This swan, frightened by canoeists on the Stour, caused chaos when it dropped into the main street until it was ushered to the safety of the pavement. The swan was collected by the RSPCA and later restored to the river.

1954 August: The open-air baths at Whitehall Road had been closed to swimmers since the war — and the pool at Kingsmead did not open until 1970. There was a long campaign for an alternative — as this 'Kingsmead Lido' float demonstrates in the carnival. The parade, only the second since the war, attracted 78 entries. The route, from Cockering Road to St Dunstan's, here passes the Thanington pumping station, itself now part of history.

1970 July: The rock group Perplexity was accused of desecrating the Boer War memorial by performing there at the Becket Festival's open-air pop concert in the Dane John, watched by about 300 people.

1954 Summer: This two-year-old bullock went berserk and ran off while being loaded into a lorry at the cattle market. It ran down Wincheap Grove and into St Mildred's churchyard before jumping into the river, where it splashed downstream — passing under the Greyfriars, the King's and Friars bridges, watched by crowds of spectators. It eventually turned back and was lassoed by drover Bill Woodman by a wooden bridge in the Tannery allotments. It survived — none the worse for its ordeal.

1952 October: Salt, a 65-year-old Ceylon elephant (with trainer Prince Abdul Karim, his wife and two sons), after she was rescued from Vauxhall lakes after a seven-hour ordeal. Salt had wandered off from her grazing ground at Sturry Road when Ringland's Circus came to town. Salt (and 55-year-old Saucy) were regular city visitors over 40 years. But this was Salt's last visit — she never recovered and died a week later.

1952 October: Wincheap County Primary School pupils held a harvest thanksgiving. Headmaster Mr C.Bradshaw thanked the children and their parents for the magnificent display of food, vegetables and groceries, which were to be sent to the bazaar in aid of the Save the Children Fund the following day.

1964 June: Anti-pigeon measures in the Longmarket went wrong. A substance smeared along the edges of roofs was intended to put the pigeons off — but birds became gummed up and fell to the ground; three pigeons and 17 starlings had to be destroyed. Here, Longmarket Traders' Association chairman Andrew Price helps cover the substance with newspaper.

1963 June: There was a plea for traffic lights at 'suicide corner'. People living on the 650-home London Road estate feared accidents after the opening of the Rheims Way a fortnight before. The only crossing was a subway farther down the road into Queen's Avenue. Only one carriageway was open at this time and the roundabout had not yet been built. Cyclists here are seen leaving Knight Avenue.

1965 February: Over the years Rootes Ltd expanded a small section of its Canterbury workshops into a thriving little industry employing over 150 staff at Rhodaus Town in premises that were originally part of Canterbury Motor Company. It made complete car seats, seat covers and other items of car trimming for the Sunbeam Rapier, Humber Sceptre and Humber Imperial.

1954 August: Miss Canterbury, 17-year-old Pauline Groombridge, on her carnival float with Maids of Honour Barbara Farrow, 16, and Shirley Mears, 16.

1969 April: Former *Kentish Gazette* chief photographer Arthur Palmer, who took many of the pictures in this book.

1969 April: Long before computers appeared on desks, this was the scene in the *Kentish Gazette* newsroom.

1955: Veteran cobbler Charles Denne, then about 80, of Sudbury Tower. His first interview with the press, recalled by Councillor John Stone (also pictured here), was when Edgar Wallace, then on the London Standard, was taken round during a visit to the city. Councillor Stone (or 'Stonie') was himself an interesting character. He died, aged 94, in 1957 — having been a city councillor since 1899.

1957 November: Marquees set up in Dane John for the Canterbury Festival Flower Show.

1958 spring: Last city wheelwright Charles Taylor, 62 (who had been with R.J.Ede and Son, motor engineers of Pound Lane, since 1911) recalled the days when cars and lorries had wooden wheels which he repaired. Mass production had taken his trade away.

1965 October: The Beatles were banned at Barham. The four dolls were among 16 that stood outside the Dolls' House on the Elham Valley Road. But Bridge-Blean RDC said they should go because they did not have planning permission. Some of the dolls had been there for 15 years. They included Andy Pandy, Looby Loo and Bill and Ben. Owner Mrs Vera Hayes said: "This is rather ridiculous."

Flooding, Fires and Bad Weather

1953 July: A violent storm flooded the Riding Gate end of Old Dover Road.

1954 June: One of the most spectacular blazes in Canterbury since the war was the fire which destroyed the Westgate flour mills of W. Hooker and Son at The Causeway. It recalled Denne's Mill blaze of October 1933.

1955 January: Courts' 18th-century showroom, store and workshops, on the corner of Butchery Lane and Burgate, was gutted by fire. The building was one of the few on that corner to escape the Blitz of 1942. Just visible behind the fire engine is the old rear entrance to the Longmarket and Corn Exchange.

1955 January: A rapid thaw of snow followed by rain caused flooding at The Causeway. Workmen demolished bridge parapets to build a bulwark of sandbags to contain water.

1961 December: Firemen from Canterbury and Sturry tackle a blaze which destroyed the staff canteen at the Tannery. It was discovered by Town Sergeant Harry Surridge, of Rosemary Lane, who was on his way to feed his two goats in St Mildred's churchyard. He tackled the fire with the Tannery's own equipment until the firemen arrived.

1962 December: Three people were treated in hospital for cuts and shock after this London-bound coach crashed into a telegraph pole in Wincheap. Snow swept over Kent on Thursday, 27 December, bringing chaos in its wake. By lunchtime there were up to six inches — and 50 snowploughs were trying to keep the roads open. The big freeze was to last several months.

1962-63: At the turn of the year, traffic policemen help recover a car from a snow drift on the Herne Bay road at Broad Oak.

1963 January: The Arctic conditions continued during the week and brought little respite to man — nor to these donkeys, which spent the winter resting on the banks of the Stour in Westgate Gardens. Behind them is the new bridge to carry the A2 diversion (Rheims Way) over the river.

1963
February:
Thawing
frozen coal
sacks over a
brazier at the
West Station
during the big
freeze.

1962 December: The day after Boxing Day, with thick snow falling, a bus passes through the Westgate.

1962 December: A double-decker bus eases its way up St Thomas's Hill in the snow.

1962 December: The thick snow quickly turned many roads ghostly silent. This was the scene at Blean.

1962 December: With Christmas barely gone, the snow made a seasonal postcard of Canterbury's skyline.

1963 January: Children build an igloo at Bossingham.

1955 January: Flooding in Westgate Gardens.

1963 March: A spectacular fire gutted the top floor of Ricemans' new £350,000 store, which had opened only the previous September. A total of 35 firemen from nine towns and villages tackled the blaze, which burnt out the Grace and Favour Restaurant, offices and the fashion theatre. The store reopened six days after the fire.

1964 May: A blaze at Courts furniture showrooms and store in Burgate. The store was built only five years before to replace another severely damaged by fire.

1970 March: The last minutes of the 136-year-old Barham windmill, destroyed by fire. The mill was gutted and the massive sails collapsed before flames could be brought under control.

Country Matters

1952 June: William Bushell, 64, found digging too much on Lord Hawarden's Ileden Farm, near Barham, so he built a mechanical two-furrow plough using the engine from a 1926 350cc Royal Enfield, bought some years before for 15 shillings.

1953 October: Sidney Keeler thatches wheat stacks at Wellbrook Farm, Boughton, helped by 75-year-old Frank Standen, to guard them against winter weather. A ton and a half of straw was used to thatch ricks like these.

1953 March: Farm horses were 'a sight becoming ever more rare,' reported the *Kentish Gazette*. Here are Dolly and Duke, with horseman Fred Cleaver, owned by Mr J.Montgomery, of Wickham Court.

1953 November: Miss June Kirk, 18, of Littlebourne, was elected the first Apple Queen of England for the East Kent Fruit Show in Canterbury. Her prizes included a frock and nylons.

1956 September: The pungent odour of incense mingled with the tang of hops and the distinctive smell of wood smoke at the 150-hut hop-pickers' camp at Mr L.Hubble's China Farm, Upper Harbledown, when Evening Mass was held. Holy Communion was conducted by the Rev Peter Spargo, of the Church of England's Temperance Society Mission to Hop-Pickers.

1954 September: A hop picking machine in action at Tony Redsell's farm at Boughton. The use of such machines grew to beat a labour shortage.

1963 September: Hop pickers at Petham, where machines had not taken over. 'It's their annual holiday — hop picking in Kent,' reported the *Kentish Gazette*.

1968 December: The dark days of winter did not hold up apple tree pruning at Mount's Little Barton Farm, Canterbury. The workers wore miners' helmets with lamps to light their way.

1960 February: Mr V.Martin, secretary-manager of the Canterbury and District Rabbit Clearance Society, watches as operator R.Boraston pumps gas into a rabbit hole. He was finding many colonies of rabbits which had survived the second epidemic of myxomatosis.

1956 July: A portable TV, run by a 12-volt battery, provided entertainment for fruit pickers at Selling.

1955 March: Minister of Agriculture Derick Heathcoat Amory (on stand, left) helps auction sheep as he opens the new Canterbury cattle market, watched by the Mayor, Alderman Harold Dawton, and Sheriff, Alderman Stanley Jennings.

1960 March: Hop stringer J.Daniels at work at Stone Star Farm, Selling.

1955 August: Harvesting at Chilham.

Church, MPs and Royalty

1944 October: The Archbishop of Canterbury, Dr William Temple, died shortly after his 63rd birthday this month. The Cathedral was crowded with 3,000 people for his funeral, which was attended by the Bishops of Rochester, Worcester, Salisbury, Winchester and London, Archbishop Lord Lang and the Archbishop of York. Before the service the coffin had been lying in state in the Chapel of Our Lady Undercroft. On the coffin was the Archbishop's pastoral staff.

1953 February: Archbishop Dr Geoffrey Fisher was presented with the freedom of the city at Simon Langton Girls' School. The Mayor, Councillor John Barrett, presents the casket containing the scroll of freedom. He was only the third of 99 Archbishops of Canterbury to receive the honour.

1953 April: Former Conservative MP John Baker White, who represented the city from 1945-53 (when he stood down because of ill health), was presented with a cocktail shaker at the annual meeting of the Divisional Conservative and Unionist Association at the Auction Room, Canterbury, by Alderman Evelyn Hews, the retiring chairman of the association. Mr Baker White died in 1988, aged 86.

1955 June: Princess Alexandra shared the celebrations at St Edmund's School on its centenary in the city and joined in the service (as patron) of Red Cross cadets in the Cathedral.

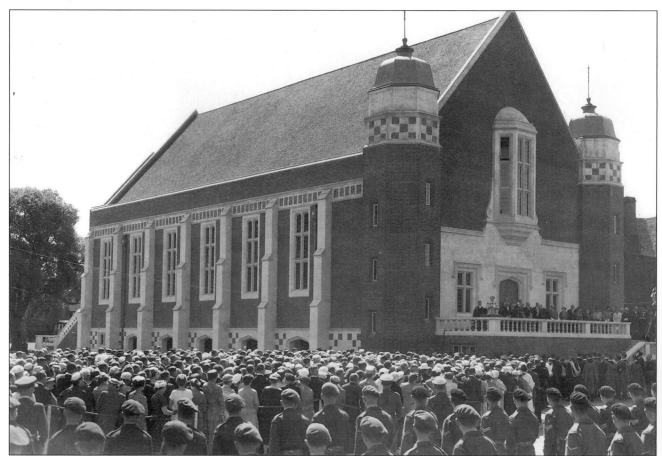

1957 June: The Queen Mother visited the King's School to open the Great Hall, now the Shirley Hall, named after the then head, Canon Frederick Shirley.

1959 October: Victorious Conservative MP Leslie Thomas (left) with returning officer John Boyle and Labour candidate George Peter (right) on the steps of the Beaney Institute when the election results were announced. His majority of 15,100 was the largest Tory majority in Kent. The MP, the son of a former Labour Cabinet minister, represented the city from 1953-66 and was knighted in 1963. He died in 1971.

1970 July: Archbishop Dr Michael Ramsey accompanies the Queen Mother to the Cathedral to attend the national service to commemorate the 800th anniversary of the Martyrdom of Thomas Becket.

1963 April: Dr Hewlett Johnson makes his way from the Deanery to the Cathedral to preach as Dean of Canterbury for the last time. Dr Johnson, a controversial figure known as the Red Dean because of his communist sympathies, had occupied the post since 1931. He died, aged 92, in 1966.

1962 July: The Queen Mother was at King's School to unveil a plaque in the Great Hall to Canon Frederick Shirley, who was retiring after 27 years as headmaster at the end of that term.

1965 April: The Queen and Duke of Edinburgh attended the Royal Maundy service, held for the first time in the Cathedral, and then toured Christ Church College. The Maundy money was presented to 39 men and 39 women — one for each year of the Queen's age. The Queen is greeted at the Westgate — the traditional entry point for important visitors — by the Mayor, Councillor Ernest Kingsman.

1964 April: Princess Marina, Duchess of Kent (seen from behind), treads carefully as she makes her first visit to the site of the University, of which she was chancellor. She said: "What a magnificent view." Foundations and drainage had been laid. That October the University's first research students arrived at Beverley Farm on the campus.

1966 March: Princess Marina, Duchess of Kent, is installed as the first Chancellor of the University of Kent at Canterbury.

1966 April: David Crouch, 46, waves at the Beaney Institute, where the count was held, after gaining an 11,788 majority to become the new Conservative MP for Canterbury — 172 more than the previous majority of Sir Leslie Thomas. The MP represented the city until 1987, in which year he was knighted.

1967 Spring: Princess Margaret, president of Dr Barnardo's, with Mayor Councillor Bernard Porter on her first official visit to the city to open the new Dr Barnardo's home, where 32 children lived in three cottages on St Thomas's Hill.

1967 November: His Holiness Athenagoras, Patriach of the Church of Constantinople, created history when he visited Canterbury as a guest of the Archbishop, Dr Michael Ramsey, to help foster church unity.

1965 April: The Queen, in Canterbury for the Royal Maundy service, toured the new Christ Church College (which had opened in October 1964) with the principal, Dr Frederic Mason.

1953 June: Queen Salote Tubou of Tonga, who was in England for the Queen's coronation, tours King's School with headmaster Canon Frederick Shirley. While in Canterbury she also visited the Cathedral.

1950 May: Princess Margaret came to Canterbury to distribute the prizes at St Edmund's School (of which her father, King George VI, was patron). The school was celebrating its bi-centenary, having moved to Canterbury from St John's Wood nearly 100 years before. Here, the Princess inspects the guard of honour at St Edmund's School, accompanied by Major Stephen Jones and headmaster William Thoseby. She also went to the Cathedral during her semi-official visit to the city.

1947 August: Princess Elizabeth leaves the Cathedral accompanied by the Archbishop, Dr Geoffrey Fisher, and the Dean, Dr Hewlett Johnson, during a semi-private visit to the city. She attended, as president, the conference of the Church of England Youth Council at King's School, followed by a special service at the Cathedral.

1961 June: A few days before his enthronement as Archbishop, Dr Michael Ramsey made his first official visit to the city for a civic reception in the Slater Hall at the Beaney Institute. He is greeted by the Mayor, Councillor Arthur Wilson.

1961 June: Those present at the enthronement of Dr Ramsey included Home Secretary R.A.Butler, Chancellor of the Exchequer Selwyn Lloyd and Hugh Gaitskell, Leader of the Opposition.

1961 June: Not only was Dr Ramsey's enthronement service televised by the BBC and ITV but closed circuit screens allowed the congregation in all parts of the Cathedral to see the ceremony.

Canterbury at War

After the Blitz of 1942 the ruins were levelled to reveal this unique view of the Cathedral, as seen from St George's Street. St Thomas's RC Church is on the right.

This post-Blitz view from the roof of Marks and Spencer looks up St George's Street towards St George's Church, by now shrouded in scaffolding.

Marks and Spencer stands alone in St George's Street, sole survivor in a row of blitzed buildings. Rose Lane is just visible (right).

Two men walk down Rose Lane, past the ruins of the Rose Hotel. Note the barrage balloon above the Cathedral.

The blitzed Royal Fountain Hotel in St Margaret's Street, now the site of the Marlowe Arcade.

Firemen hose down smoking rubble in June 1942. Marks and Spencer (left) was left standing amid the ruins.

This 1940 view of the old Corn Exchange and Longmarket building in St George's Street clearly shows the War Savings indicator on its frontage. *Picture: Fisk-Moore.*

Hose pipes snake across St George's Street in front of the Corn Exchange after the Blitz. *Picture: Fisk-Moore.*

Although the Corn Exchange building was gutted in the raid its shell survived, as this wartime picture clearly shows.

The Duke of Kent (in uniform, centre) with the Mayor, Alderman Charles Lefevre, outside the ruins of the Rose Hotel. The Duke, who was serving with the RAF, toured the city on 4 June. Two months later he was killed in a plane crash in Scotland.

Watling Street was hit badly in the raid of October 1942. Riding Gate bridge can be seen in the distance; the building on the right is the Dane John Tavern.

The ruins of Lady Wootton's Green after the Blitz.

The Dean of Canterbury, Dr Hewlett Johnson, surveys the ruins of the bombed Cathedral Library.

Although the worst damage in Canterbury occurred in 1942, bombs fell on Burgate in October 1940. Iron Bar Lane is left; the old rear entrance to the Longmarket is just visible (right).

The bombed ruins of St Mary Bredin Church, viewed from Rose Lane. A day or two later, the weather-boarded building on the right was destroyed in a smaller June raid.

A barrage balloon at its moorings in the Green Court at King's School.

ATC Cadets in the Salute the Soldier parade in Canterbury in May 1944. They are seen walking up the High Street past the old Guildhall on the corner of Guildhall Street.

Tons of soil were dumped in the Nave of the Cathedral before being used in the building for protective work.

The Mayor, Mrs Catherine Williamson (accompanied by Chief Constable T.Hall), inspects members of the city police force with contingents of the Auxiliary Fire Service and other ARP units before a church parade in April 1940.

"Well done! The nation is proud of you," said the Duchess of Kent to 1,700 Kent Land Girls at a march past and presentation at the St Lawrence Ground on 29 June 1945.

Children race for cover during air raid drill. This shelter was in St Peter's Place, opposite the then bus station.

The casualty list outside the Beaney Institute in the High Street made grim reading after the raids of 1942. The three attacks in June killed 49 people, while another 32 people died in the main October raid.

Troops demonstrate their readiness for battle during an exercise in the shadow of the Westgate in St Peter's Street in late October 1941. The joint manoeuvres between the Civil Defence, the Home Guard and the Army involved the 'capture' of the East and West railway stations and fierce 'street fighting' at the Westgate itself.

Soldiers help a rescue party amid the rubble in Lower Bridge Street. The trees at the old cattle market site can be seen in the distance.

Looking down blitzed St George's Place from its junction with Lower Chantry Lane.

Damage was not confined to the centre of Canterbury. Houses on the Thanington estate were also destroyed in 1942.

Looting signs in Canterbury warned of the penalties.

King's School was damaged in the June raids but the Norman staircase, although battered, survived.

The Dean, Dr Hewlett Johnson, receives help in salvaging books from the bombed Cathedral Library in June 1942.

The ruins of Rose Lane after the Blitz of June 1942.

The ruined garage of E.J.Philpott Ltd in Rose Lane after the raid of October 1942.

The smoking ruins of the city, as seen from the Cathedral on 1 June 1942 — the morning after the worst bombing of Canterbury in the war. The Corn Exchange and Longmarket building and Marks and Spencer can be seen in the centre. *Picture: Anthony Swaine.*

A work party digs amid the rubble of a bombed building in Wincheap after the second Blitz of Canterbury in October/November.

Helped by rescue squads, residents try to salvage some of their belongings in Nunnery Fields after the raid of October 1942.

The village centre of Sturry was devastated in November 1941, when two parachute mines fell on it, killing 15 people.

Mrs Eleanor Roosevelt, wife of the president of the United States, with the Mayor of Canterbury, Alderman Charles Lefevre, outside the Cathedral on 30 October 1942. She was visiting the city with Mrs Churchill. The following day Canterbury suffered its second worst bombing raid of the war.

Looking down York Road towards Wincheap after the second Blitz. Grove Terrace is on the right.

Boorman's the butchers at the corner of Broad Street and Church Street St Paul's was badly damaged in the Blitz — but survived to carry on trading.

The Duke of Kent (right) walks past the ruins of St George's Church on his tour of the blitzed city. His party included the Mayor, Alderman Charles Lefevre, and (behind him) the Dean, Dr Hewlett Johnson.

Red Cross, Police and Civil Defence workers pass the blitzed ruins of St George's Church in the Wings for Victory parade in April 1943.

More than 3,000 Home Guard officers and members attended the official stand-down service in the Cathedral in October 1944. Lord Cornwallis, Lord Lieutenant of Kent, took the salute in the Broad Street car park. In the distance are the gables of the Saracen's Head in Burgate, demolished in 1969 for the ring road.

NFS firemen take time out for a cuppa in Canterbury in January 1944.

A battalion of the Home Guard marches through the Westgate in March 1941.

People in Artillery Street celebrate the end of war in Europe in May 1945.

The people of Guelph (Ontario, Canada) presented a mobile canteen to their 'brave brothers and sisters' in Canterbury. The presentation ceremony at the Poor Priests' Hospital in Stour Street was attended by the Mayor, Alderman Charles Lefevre, and Mr F. Hudd, Official Secretary for Canada House.

1943 September: Familiar scenes were recorded this year when *A Canterbury Tale* was filmed in and around the blitzed city. Here, the four stars — Sgt John Sweet, of the US Army, Eric Portman, Sheila Sim and Dennis Price — meet for the first time on location at Breeden Hill, Chilham. Director Michael Powell (right) was born at Bekesbourne. The world premiere was held at the Friars Theatre (now the Marlowe) in May 1944.

1945 June: German prisoners-of-war excavate a sewer trench at Westgate Court Avenue ready for prefabs to be built there.

Famous Faces

1967 November: Comedian Jimmy Tarbuck leads a Showbiz XI on to the field at Kingsmead on 5 November for a charity match against past and present Canterbury City players. His team included ex-Spurs and Northern Ireland international Danny Blanchflower and Ray Davies of the Kinks. Canterbury won 7-5 (with Tarbuck having scored two goals).

1953 July: Eamonn Andrews interviews two Americans (Mr and Mrs David Morris) in the Cathedral Precincts for the BBC programme *Welcome to Britain*.

1954 November: Radio and film star Jack Warner (who was to become more famous in the title role of *Dixon of Dock Green*) presented the awards at the Kent National Open Show, organised by the Canterbury and District Cage Bird Society, at the Drill Hall (later the Westgate Hall).

1954 August: Kenneth More, at the wheel of the car, asks Councillor A.Ross, farmer and chairman of Bridge-Blean RDC, for directions at Barham windmill. Councillor Ross played a countryman for the scene in the film *Raising a Riot*, which centres on a naval officer who tries to cope with his three lively children while staying with his elderly father in a derelict windmill.

1958 May: Alan Whicker, of BBC TV's *Tonight* programme, interviews Miss M.Sheehan, matron of Kent and Canterbury Hospital's Stodmarsh Road annexe — the opening of which had been delayed because of difficulties in finding domestic staff.

1962 June: Judy Garland and Dirk Bogarde were in the Cathedral Precincts to film a few scenes for *The Lonely Stage* (actually released as *I Could Go On Singing*), directed by Michael Neame. But the 87-year-old Dean, Dr Hewlett Johnson, took exception to a group of 'scruffy and untidy' extras dressed to look like King's School pupils. School captain Michael Morpurgo had been concerned at the boys' long hair and suede winkle pickers.

1961 September: TV personality Hughie Green — who died in 1997 — opens an exhibition of furniture and household equipment at Jays Furnishing Stores, St George's Street. Police controlled a 'huge crowd' which blocked the pavements on both sides of the street for half an hour before he arrived.

1961 October: King's School old boy Somerset Maugham, then 88, returned to Canterbury to open a £5,000 library he gave to the school to house the collection of rare books and manuscripts he was leaving in his will. He is accompanied by headmaster Canon Frederick Shirley and head boy Michael Morpurgo.

1964 February: Actress Jane Asher, 17, poses by the Marlowe memorial (then in Dane John). She was in Canterbury to star in *The Jew of Malta*, the play by Christopher Marlowe being produced at the old Marlowe Theatre to mark the 400th anniversary of his birth. Jane Asher was then the girlfriend of Beatle Paul McCartney. During the play's run — and with Beatlemania at its height — McCartney was smuggled into the theatre by *Kentish Gazette* staff one night so that he could watch her performance unrecognised.

1963 September: Disc jockey David Jacobs reopens the top floor at Ricemans after the spectacular fire in March of that year.

1964 Summer: Kim Novak was in Chilham to film *The Amorous Adventures of Moll Flanders*. There was filming inside the castle, the Square and castle grounds. It also starred George Sanders, Angela Lansbury and Leo McKern. The Square was transformed into an 18th-century market for this scene.

1965 October: Miss World, 21-year-old Ann Sidney, came to Canterbury to compère a wool fashion parade at Ricemans — where two years before she had had her first modelling assignment.

1964 April: Steptoe Snr (alias Wilfred Brambell) escorts actress Julia Foster to the ABC Cinema for the provincial premiere of *Becket*. Other guests included Ronald Fraser and Charles Hawtry. The gala raised £2,000 for the NSPCC.

1966 May: The Kinks were the main attraction of the rag ball at the University.

1969 November: Peter Firmin (left) and Oliver Postgate at work on the children's TV programme *The Clangers* in their Blean studio.

1971 April: Joanna Lumley — pictured on the roof of the old Marlowe Theatre in St Margaret's Street — was in the theatre's cast of *Not Now Darling*. Another member of the theatre company that season was the actress Jane Seymour.

1930 September: Lord Baden-Powell, passing the old Guildhall in Guildhall Street, was in Canterbury to receive the Freedom of the City. He is accompanied by District Commissioner S.Haynes.

1959 May: Southern Auto's 'revolutionary open plan' motor service station and showroom opened in Rose Lane. To mark the occasion, Jack Warner — the first 'customer' — arrived there in Chitty Bang Bang, once the pride of Count Zabrowski's fleet of racing cars. Here, Jack Warner poses in the car outside the Chaucer Hotel. Count Zabrowski, who raced for Mercedes, used to live at Highland Court, Bridge. It was there that he built the car made famous by the film it inspired.

Farewell to the Old

1967 February: Prefabs being demolished in the Churchill Road area of New Dover Road.

1961 December: The 400-year-old ferry on the Stour at Grove was being replaced by a new £24,000 bridge. It was then one of the few remaining ferries in the country. Here, the ferry crosses the river alongside the half-built bridge.

1960 July: Queues at Canterbury Post Office were not uncommon — in part, at least, because people had to queue at different counters for different service. But after this picture was taken the system changed and specific counters became a thing of the past.

1952 December: 'With the engine whistle sounding a continuous death wail' the last train on the Canterbury to Whitstable railway puffed slowly from Whitstable Harbour on its final journey to Canterbury West (above). Rolling into the station for the last time, a series of fog detonators recalled the firing of a cannon from the Westgate which marked the departure of the first train 122 years before. A 60-year-old engine hauled two brake vans back to Whitstable. But within a few months the line was (temporarily) called into service again — to take coal to Whitstable when its main line was cut off by the severe flooding of February 1953. The line issued the world's first railway season tickets in 1834.

1955 January: Workmen demolish the Riding Gate Inn. It was badly damaged during the war and used since only as a lock-up.

1962 August: Rebuilt after bomb damage in the war, this 20-yard section of the city wall near Riding Gate collapsed.

1957 August: Workmen remove one of the two chimneys on the old St Dunstan's brewery, then being converted for light industry. In the foreground is the Roper Gateway.

1959 January: Only one of the original 'Seven Sisters' — pylons at the old RAF radar station at Dunkirk — was left after three of the remaining four were felled by gelignite. The last was spared for use by the BBC.

1959 February: 'Sub-standard' property in Union Street is torn down as part of the city council's largest slum clearance scheme.

1959 October: The 130-foot-high chimney at Kingsmead Road, built in 1900 for the Canterbury Electricity Works' hand-fired boilers, being demolished.

1964 June: There was anger at the conversion of part of Millers Field playground into a car park. The field had been presented to the city council by Frank Hooker in 1929 'as a playing field for the specific use of children in the North Lane and Northgate area'. The field was opposite The Causeway site of the Hooker mill, destroyed by fire in 1954.

1965 September: The oldest part of Canterbury Prison, the original jailhouse built in 1808, is demolished to make way for a new reception building and administration section.

1970 October: The mid-Victorian Riding Gate bridge is lifted away by a crane to make way for a new pedestrian walk along the city walls. The bridge ended up in Heathfield Wildlife Park, Sussex.

Previous page: 1965 September: The last three lime kilns at Frank Cooper Ltd's lime works at south Canterbury were being demolished. The works closed the previous year. Modern building methods and materials had left lime production a dying art. But after 30 years of burning night and day at a temperature of 3,000F the kilns had fused into solid blocks — making the job of knocking them down difficult.

1951 February: By this date the old Guildhall, the victim of decay, had been demolished to ground floor level.

1955 March: The demolition of the old Elham Valley Line railway bridge by Hollow Lane at Wincheap. The line itself closed in 1947.

1959 January: The end of an era. A steam train at Canterbury East — in the year the London to Dover line was electrified.

1952 June: Canterbury said goodbye to four British Rail horses which had become a familiar sight in the city's streets. Jinny, Big Charlie, Brown Charlie and Darkie lost their jobs to lorries.

Sport, Leisure, Recreation

Kent and England cricketer Alfred Percy ('Tich') Freeman in action. During cricket week in 1931 he took 15 wickets for 94 runs in a match against Somerset — still the best match analysis for Kent. Freeman took 3,340 wickets for the county, far more than anyone else and the second highest by anyone in the history of cricket. Freeman, who bowled leg spinners and was known as Tich because he was little more than five feet tall, played 506 matches for Kent from 1914-36. He died in 1965, aged 76.

1946 May: Before the start of the Kent v Yorkshire game at the St Lawrence Ground — in the first home county championship match since the war — both team captains (Bryan Valentine and Arthur Sellers) placed wreaths on the war memorial to the Kent players and led a silent tribute while lined up alongside the playing pitch. Kent went on to lose the match by an innings and 91 runs. The Kent team comprised (from left, after the umpire): Claude Lewis (12th man), Peter Sunnucks, Doug Wright, Tom Spencer, Norman Harding, Godfrey Evans, David Clark, Jack Martin, Tom Pearce, Leslie Todd, Leslie Ames and Bryan Valentine. The ground remained in playing condition during the war and club matches were played there, even though the Army was in occupation.

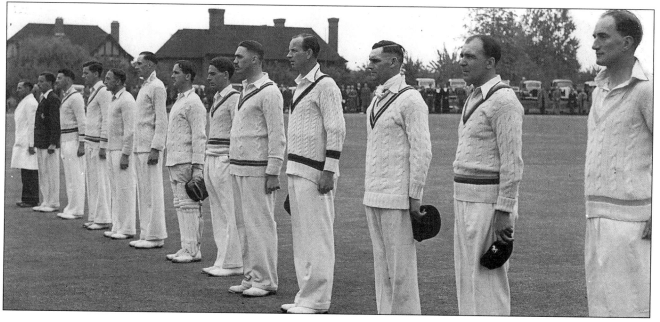

1933: Cricket Week at the St Lawrence Ground, held the first week in August, is always a popular social affair. Here, crowds gather against a backdrop of tents lining the ground, which was opened in 1847.

1953 August: Kent and England wicketkeeper Godfrey Evans leads out the team to field against Hampshire in his benefit match. The game was drawn, with Kent 23 runs short of victory with the last pair in when stumps were drawn. Collections at the ground during the first two days raised £374.

1953 August: Godfrey Evans, who pitched the first ball, is initiated into the mysteries of baseball by two of the Manston Cats in their game against the Snowdown Magpies at the St Lawrence Ground.

1959 August: Crowds line the St Lawrence Ground for Cricket Week, when Kent battled with Hampshire and Derbyshire. It was not a good week for Kent — who lost to Hampshire by eight wickets and to Derbyshire by 99 runs.

1963 August: Frank Woolley, then 76, the former Kent and England all-rounder, speaks at the unveiling of a plaque to him at the St Lawrence Ground. The plaque was unveiled by Lord Nugent, president of the MCC. Frank Woolley died in October 1978.

1964 Summer: 'Gubby' Allen (right), president of the MCC, at the St Lawrence Ground unveiling of a plaque recording the highlights in the career of Leslie Ames (left). Ames, a great wicketkeeper and batsman for Kent and England, made his 100th century in the Kent v Middlesex match during Cricket Week in 1950 — and 78 of his centuries were for Kent. Ames was also a successful administrator for Kent CCC as secretary, manager or both. On his active retirement he was honoured by the club presidency in 1975.

1965 December: Father Christmas (umpire Sid Burton) watches J. Worrell on his way to take six wickets for Sturry, as Canterbury Choughs batsman Malcolm Longley looks on. The Boxing Day cricket match at Sturry was in aid of the League of Friends of Canterbury Hospitals. Sturry won and over £21 was raised.

1967 July: Kent captain Colin Cowdrey — Man of the Match — acknowledges the applause of the crowd at the St Lawrence Ground as he walks back to the pavilion after a great innings of 78 in the Gillette Cup semi-final against Sussex. Kent beat Sussex by 118 runs to get to the Final at Lord's. Cowdrey was finally bowled by Tony Greig with only one over remaining, having scored 78 off 59 balls, including 12 fours. The game is remembered as one of the best Canterbury matches to this day — the roads were packed for miles around. Kent went on to beat Somerset by 32 runs in the Final.

1968: Perhaps one of the strongest post-war teams ever fielded by Kent CCC. The captain was Colin Cowdrey, who made his first appearance for Kent at the age of 17 in 1950. The team also included Derek Underwood (debut 1963), whose total of 1,951 wickets for Kent was exceeded only by Tich Freeman; and Alan Knott (debut 1964), England's finest post-war wicketkeeper-batsman. Left to right, back: Leslie Ames (secretary-manager), John Shepherd, Derek Underwood, Norman Graham, John Dye, Asif Iqbal, Alan Knott, Claude Lewis (scorer); front: Brian Luckhurst, Dave Sayer, Alan Dixon, Colin Cowdrey, Stuart Leary, Alan Brown, Mike Denness. Kent finished second to Yorkshire in the County Championship in 1968 — their really great years were soon to follow.

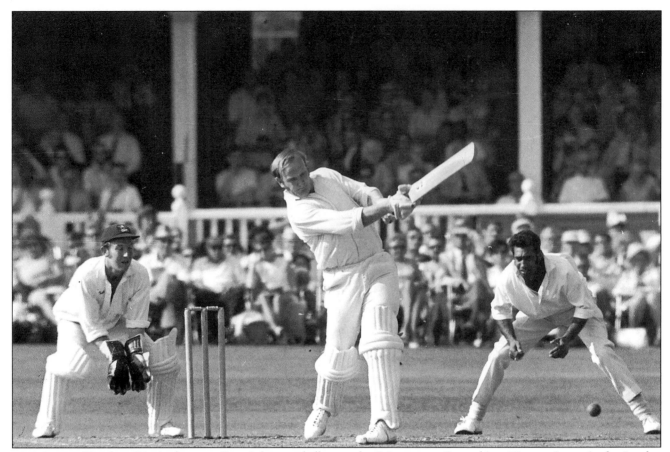

1970 August: Kent beat Nottingham — Gary Sobers and all — at the St Lawrence Ground in a 52-run victory in the Sunday League. This picture shows John Dye, one of the leading pace bowlers of the side for several years, in a rare excursion to the crease as batsman. He made two not out — and later took three wickets. Kent were denied the John Player Trophy when Lancashire beat Yorkshire. But in this, the club's, centenary year Kent went on to win the County Championship for the first time since 1913, captained by Colin Cowdrey. The centenary was marked by an appeal to raise money to rebuild the pavilion, renamed after the late chairman Stuart Chiesman (Cowdrey's father-in-law).

1958 May: The 600-spectator stand takes shape at Kingsmead Stadium, where the task of laying 30,048 turves was nearing completion.

1958 August: Kingsmead Stadium was played in for the first time here when Canterbury City beat Ashford Town 3-2, watched in 'torrid heat' by a shirt-sleeved crowd of 2,300. It was officially opened a few days later on Thursday, 4 September by Sir Stanley Rous, secretary of the Football Association, when City were at home to Kent League champions Sittingbourne. That game was drawn 1-1.

1964 January: Coventry City manager Jimmy Hill (fourth left) at a Canterbury Football Club meeting after a £5,000 appeal had been launched to bring floodlighting to Kingsmead.

1964 August: The last of the floodlight pylons goes up at Kingsmead Stadium.

1964 November: There was FA Cup defeat when Canterbury (in striped shirts) lost at home to Fourth Division Torquay United 6-0. A crowd of 3,000 was then the biggest at Kingsmead to watch Canterbury — who had been waiting 16 years to meet Football League opponents again.

1958 October: The hula hoop craze got under way in Canterbury with a demonstration at the Odeon cinema in The Friars (now the Marlowe Theatre). Girls swayed hoops round their bodies to the music of the 20-piece Old Age Pensioners' skiffle group. Imported from America, the craze was then sweeping the country.

1960 May: The 'most popular amusement' at the Prince of Wales Youth Club was jiving.

1967 April: Grand National runner 13-year-old Bob-a-Job, owned and trained by Tom Hudson, of Upper Thruxted Farm, Chartham. His jockey was 18-year-old Chris Young. Bob-a-Job was in the middle of the leading group when a pile-up and a loose horse forced him to make three attempts at a fence. He was officially placed 12th.

1966 August: A scorching weekend — and Canterbury's youngsters took full advantage of it at Toddlers Cove. Note the old swimming pool, then being used for boating.

1968 May: A crowd of 7,000 people, then the biggest ever at Kingsmead Stadium, turned out to see speedway come to Canterbury. They watched the city's first British League (Division Two) match between Canterbury Crusaders and the Bell Vue (Manchester) Babes. Canterbury lost by 38 points to 39.

1954 August: The Final of the Canterbury bat and trap Festival Cup tournament was held in Dane John. Canterbury British Legion (who won the trophy) bat against the Post Office Telephones.

1953 September: 'The Littlebourne Lido. No need to go to the seaside when the Lesser Stour is available,' reported the *Kentish Gazette*.

1954 May: Grandmother Elizabeth Twinning, 71, of St Radigund's Street, a star of the Dolphin pub team, reckoned she must have been one of the oldest bat and trap players in the world.

1954 May: Ted Long, 74, a member of the White Hart bat and trap home team, faces the cameras. The team was playing Dolphin 'B' under the gaze of reporter Douglas Brown, from *Radio Newsreel*.

1955 August: Children flock to Westgate Gardens, where donkey rides were in great demand.

1960 May: Members of the East Kent Federation of Women's Institutes enjoy an afternoon of country dancing in the Deanery Gardens.

1955 April: Easter Monday's sunshine brought out the holidaymakers to Tower Gardens. It was, said the *Kent Herald*, reminiscent of wartime 'holidays at home' when these gardens were a favoured spot.

Inside the Walls

Although this picture was taken before 1930 — it dates from early in the century — it clearly shows how St George's Street used to look before the Blitz destroyed the church and the buildings round it. *Picture: Courtesy Paul Crampton.*

1957 January: Looking down St George's Street. The corner of St George's Lane (where McDonald's is now) had yet to be developed.

1953 March: The church of St Mary de Castro disappeared centuries ago — but its churchyard survives as a small oasis of green off Castle Street.

1940s: The rear entrance gate to the old Longmarket and Corn Exchange in Burgate. It survived the Blitz but was demolished in the late 1950s.

1930s: Part of the original 1881 Simon Langton schools which used to dominate the Whitefriars area between St George's Street and Gravel Walk. The girls moved out after the buildings were damaged by wartime bombing. But the boys remained until 1959.

1940: Looking along Stour Street towards St Mildred's Church. Beasley's dyeworks was damaged in the Blitz but the building survived until the early 1960s.

1954 January: The Georgian tower of St Andrew's Church in The Parade, which was demolished in 1956. The site is now part of NatWest Bank.

1954 January: Workmen put up 25ft-tall lamp standards to replace older ones. Behind them, the post-war Longmarket still awaits redevelopment.

1955 June: Only a month after the foundation stone was laid, rapid progress was being made at the £70,000 bus station in St George's Lane. Ricemans had yet to be built.

1956 May: The bus station is now in full operation. A Watling Street exit was then being used temporarily and was to be repositioned when St George's Lane was made a dual carriageway after Simon Langton School (visible on the left) had moved.

1956 July: The new National Provincial Building at the Longmarket. The old bank was blitzed in 1942 and carried on trading in a temporary brick building. The bank's original architect wanted a building in the classical style — but Canterbury council wanted a 'contemporary design'. This building was demolished in 1996.

1955 February: The David Greig building of 1953 won architects Robert Paine and Partners a RIBA Bronze Medal — even though the year it opened the Archbishop, Dr Geoffrey Fisher, described it as a monstrosity. It is now part of Woolworths.

1963 June: Renovation continued at Ricemans after the spectacular fire of March that year, when the top floor was badly damaged.

1958 December: Parked cars in St Margaret's Street, then one-way, illustrated problems over parking in the city centre. The gap on the left, then being used as a car park, was the site of the blitzed Royal Fountain Hotel.

1965 January: Traffic on the King's Bridge, which was described by some as a dangerous bottleneck.

1968 February: Before the multi-storey car park was built (as this view from the Bell Harry tower of the Cathedral shows) the areas behind St George's Street were dominated by open-air car parks.

1969 August: Traffic in the High Street passes the old Baldwin and Son store.

1955 May: Work begins on the new bus station site in St George's Lane.

1934: Nason's, now in the High Street, began life at the corner of Castle Street and St Mary's Street.

1964 December: A floodlit Cathedral rises above the city skyline, as seen from The Friars.

1965 Autumn: Looking down Gravel Walk towards Rose Lane, before the building of the multi-storey car park and the Whitefriars complex.

1942: A bus passes a horse and cart in the High Street. The Guildhall (right), once the home of city council meetings, was demolished in 1950-51 — even though some felt it could have been repaired and saved.

Abbot's Mill, which was on the corner of Mill Lane and St Radigund's Street, opposite the Millers Arms pub, rises above the skyline in this view from The Causeway. The mill was destroyed by fire in October 1933.

1959 February: The Longmarket begins to take shape, although prefabricated shops are still in use (left).

1951 December: The old Marlowe Theatre in St Margaret's Street. It was built in 1927, originally as the Central Picture Theatre, and demolished in 1982 to make way for the Marlowe Arcade.

1952 September: Post-war St George's Street is evolving but the old Simon Langton School still dominates the Whitefriars area and the Longmarket is still occupied by prefab shops.

1957 March: Looking down Burgate towards the Buttermarket. The blitzed Iron Bar Lane and Longmarket sites still await redevelopment.

1954 July: St George's Clocktower after post-war repairs had been completed and the scaffolding removed. The area around it was still awaiting development but by this time the David Greig shop (now part of Woolworth) was open.

1957 November: This was the scene of devastation after tents erected for the East Kent Fruit and Gardeners' Society Show on the Watling Street car park were flattened by a gale. Note the buildings on the right, which were at the junction of Rose Lane and Watling Street and were subsequently demolished for redevelopment and road widening.

1969 December: After the war the blitzed land around the old Marlowe Theatre in St Margaret's Street (which included the site of the Royal Fountain Hotel and St Mary Bredin Church) was used as an open-air car park. This view looks across the junction of Gravel Walk with Rose Lane towards St Margaret's Church, now The Canterbury Tales. The rear of the old Marlowe is just visible (left) — but the development of the site for the Marlowe Arcade was more than a decade away.

1957 November: St Peter's Place was a quiet cul-de-sac before the ring road was built. It is now a busy link from the Westgate to the Rheims Way.

1953 November: Looking up St Peter's Street from the Westgate. The electricity showrooms on the corner, demolished in 1961 for road widening that never came, used to be the Corner House Cafe. Just visible (right) are the destinations of the East Kent Road Car Company, whose bus station was in St Peter's Place until the mid-1950s.

1961 August: Depending on your point of view, the 'shoe box' building which dominated the post-war redevelopment of the Longmarket was either an eyesore which blocked out the Cathedral — or a building which provided tantalising glimpses of it. The adjoining cafe used the open-air terrace next to it for its customers.

1970 February: Arguably the ugliest and most criticised building in Canterbury's history — the multi-storey car park between Gravel Walk and Watling Street, which opened a few months earlier. It was originally planned to be two floors higher. This is the view from St George's Lane.

1968 December: Councillors inspect progress at the Watling Street multi-storey car park.

Civic and Ceremonial

1953 November: The Mayor, Alderman Harold Dawton, takes the Remembrance Day parade salute at the Cenotaph on the site of St Mary Bredman's Church (by Nason's).

1953 May: Part of the procession of over 100 banners of East Kent branches of the Mothers' Union about to enter the Cathedral for a festival service.

1957 November: Alderman Mrs Evelyn Hews CBE was presented with the freedom of the city at Simon Langton Girls' School — the first woman to receive that honour. She was first elected to the council 21 years before and was Mayor from 1946-49. She receives her freedom casket from the Mayor, Alderman William Bean.

1955 May: Women Civil Defence volunteers from the Bridge-Blean area prepare stew in a compound behind the municipal buildings at Canterbury (then at Dane John) for an exercise involving 50 men. It was served in a gravel pit at Bigberry Woods, Chartham Hatch.

1955 September: About 12,000 Roman Catholics came to Canterbury for the pilgrimage in honour of St Thomas More and the English Martyrs in one of the largest gatherings for years. The pilgrims formed a vast congregation in Dane John, where the preacher was the Very Rev W.Harty, of New Orleans, USA.

1956 March: Realism was added to a Civil Defence exercise when the men were given the chance to help demolish an old cottage in North Lane.

1963 June: The Mayor of Rheims, M.Taittinger, unveils the Rheims Way sign on Canterbury's 'new road', watched by city engineer J.Rhodes, Town Clerk John Boyle, Town Sergeant E.Roberts, Deputy Mayor Councillor E.Brown and Mayor Councillor Ernest Kingsman. The road had been in use since Whitsun.

1963 June: The scene in the Chapter House in the Cathedral when the Mayor, Councillor Ernest Kingsman (sitting, right of table), officially welcomed the Rheims delegation — twinning had been cemented the previous year when a delegation from Canterbury visited Rheims in May. Standing is the Mayor of Rheims, M.Taittinger.

1964 February: A plaque was unveiled at St George's Clocktower to commemorate the christening there of Christopher Marlowe on 26 February 1564. There was also a procession along the city wall to the newly-restored Marlowe memorial in Dane John, where wreaths were laid. Other celebrations included a concert of Elizabethan music, a banquet at the County Hotel and a service at the Cathedral.

1968 April: The final meeting and 'stand down' ceremony of the Canterbury and Bridge-Blean Corps of the Civil Defence — officially disbanded by the Government from 1 April — made it the end of an era for many volunteer members. Councillor A.Apps, chairman of the Canterbury Civil Defence Committee, said the great experience and skills of the Civil Defence had provided an insurance against the threat of civil disaster.

1968 April: Archbishop Dr Michael Ramsey went to welcome an expected 5,000 people at a Good Friday Human Rights pilgrimage at Kingsmead — but only 800 youngsters and a few adults turned up. Laziness was blamed by one of the organisers.

1953 June: Celebrations to mark the Queen's coronation on 2 June included this pageant along the city wall by Dane John mound. Here, Queen Elizabeth I (Lady Ampthill) is on the way to address her troops at Tilbury. The pageant was meant to illustrate Canterbury's connection with the Crown through the ages — but the watching crowds, particularly on the second day, were much smaller than expected and the city wall, some felt, dwarfed the spectacle for those watching from below.

1953 June: The floodlit mound in Dane John is decorated with a giant crown for the pageant along the city wall to celebrate the Queen's coronation.

1953: Enjoying a coronation dance at Kingston.

1953: Smiling faces all round at this street party in New Town Street to mark the coronation.

1957 May: The Mayor, Councillor William Bean, and Sheriff, Councillor Peter Wood, take the salute at St George's Clocktower during the annual Commonwealth Youth Sunday parade after a service at the Cathedral.

1955 September: The *Last Post* is sounded at the Battle of Britain parade at the Buttermarket war memorial.

1961 July: Tricars enter the Nave of the Cathedral for their annual Invalid Tricycle Association service. St John Ambulance Brigade members manhandled the vehicles down a special ramp and lined them up in rows, each with a cardboard square underneath to catch oil drips.

1957 Summer: The farewell dinner of the 4th (St Augustine's) Battn, Kent Home Guard — a last supper on the eve of their disbandment — was held at the Cafe Royal, Tankerton. The Battalion included a large part of the Bridge-Blean area, Whitstable and Herne Bay. About 40 men had remained active on the reserve roll.

1954 November: William Deedes, Parliamentary Secretary to the Ministry of Housing and Local Government (and MP for Ashford from 1950-74), opens one of the 'experimental' houses on the London Road estate, watched by the Mayor, Alderman Harold Dawton, and Councillor Peter Wood, chairman of the housing committee. The houses incorporated prefabricated panels.

1960 June: The end-of-term service at St Augustine's College was held in the Abbey ruins. Priest-students from all parts of the world took part. Note the former Kent and Canterbury Hospital building in Longport looming up behind. The college was then the central training college for the Anglican communion.

1954 October: This oak casket was presented to Lord Baden-Powell when he received the Freedom of the City in 1930 and had been kept at the Boy Scouts' Association HQ in London. Here, it is presented at Tower House to the Mayor of Canterbury, Alderman Harold Dawton, who accepted it on behalf of the Scouts of Kent.

1959 May: Minutes after this picture was taken Councillor Gilbert Kennett, 66 — seen (standing, left) thanking the council on his election as Sheriff of Canterbury — collapsed and was pronounced dead after being taken to Kent and Canterbury Hospital. His appearance at the council's annual meeting at the Slater Art Gallery was his first in public for several months, during which time he had been seriously ill.

Hello to the New

1965 March: The city made musical history in the 1960s with the development of what became known as the Canterbury Scene (or Sound). At its heart were the Wilde Flowers, a group whose line-up included three ex-Simon Langton Boys' School pupils — Brian Hopper, 22 (left), his brother Hugh, 19 (second right), and Robert (Wyatt) Ellidge, 20 (centre). The line-up — taken two months after their debut gig at the Bear and Key Hotel, Whitstable — is completed by Richard Sinclair, 16 (second left) and Kevin Ayers, 20 (right).

1965 October: Canterbury venues for the Wilde Flowers in their first year included The Beehive Club in Dover Street (a regular haunt), the College of Art, Prince of Wales Youth Club, Frank Hooker School, St Thomas' Hall and Canterbury Jazz and Folk Festival at Kingsmead Stadium. They also played Saturday morning gigs at the ABC Cinema, fitting in about four songs between children's films — and being paid with six months worth of complimentary tickets for Saturday night shows. Here, Brian and Hugh Hopper and Robert Wyatt (as he became known) prepare to leave the cinema to tour the city in a Mini Moke to promote the Dave Clark film *Catch Us If You Can*.

1968 September: Robert Wyatt and Kevin Ayers soon left the Wilde Flowers to form Soft Machine a group whose line-up included another ex-Simon Langton pupil, Mike Ratledge, and David Allen, an Australian on the Canterbury scene. In 1968 Richard Sinclair (back, left) and two later Wilde Flowers — his cousin David Sinclair (front, left) and Pye Hastings (back, right) — were joined by Richard Coughlan (front, right) to form Caravan. Here the band is pictured on top of Dane John mound to publicise their forthcoming album *Caravan*, released the following month.

1968 October: Although their reputation was growing, Caravan took to living in tents in a field at Graveney for a while — to be close to the village hall next door where they were rehearsing. Left to right, Richard Sinclair, David Sinclair, Richard Coughlan and Pye Hastings practise in the open air. Caravan has continued over the years (at different times and with different line-ups). The Canterbury Scene, meanwhile, gave birth to a number of other groups, most notably Camel, Matching Mole and Hatfield and the North — and the Canterbury Scene now even has its own Internet Web site (Calyx).

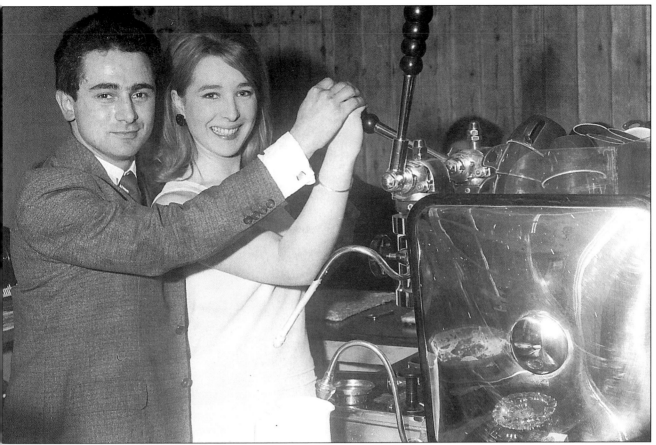

1965 May: Italian-born Franco Bevan — helped by Marlowe actress Lynne Ashcroft — opens Canterbury's new nightclub, the Beehive in Dover Street. There were three rooms where members could dance, talk or drink coffee. The club was one of the venues used by the Wilde Flowers.

1964 July: The Sheriff of Canterbury, Councillor Arthur Wilson, makes the city's first Subscriber Trunk Dialling call, watched by telephone manager C.Kent. Councillor Wilson, chairman of the council's Marlowe Theatre Committee, was calling actor Bernard Miles at the Mermaid Theatre in London. Councillor Wilson regretted that STD calling would mean less contact with the switchboard operators.

1965 February: 'Something never seen before in Canterbury,' reported the *Kentish Gazette*. An 'Off-Beat Youth Service' in St Mary Bredin Church heard Top 10 tunes such as *I'll Never Find Another You* and *Downtown* accompany the hymns. The curate, the Rev John Barton, looks on.

1964 October: The University was still a year away from opening. But this month 11 research students arrived at Beverley Farm on the campus, where temporary labs had been set up, to prepare experiments for use by the eventual undergraduates. Here, Roger Figgins, 22, adjusts an electromagnet.

1952 Summer: Students at Canterbury College of Art wear some of their own creations at their fashion parade.

1962 September: Unwary motorists were caught in this radar speed trap at Bridge. Nearly 30 drivers were stopped for speeding — but were let off with a warning.

1970 March: Chartham Primary School pupils set up shop during a decimal currency exhibition and invited their mothers along for a lesson. Decimal currency, the cause of apprehension for many people, was introduced in February 1971.

1961 March: Customers at Grafton's fashion shop in St George's Street had a chance to plan their 1961 wardrobe when models paraded the year's collection.

1964 Summer: Canterbury's new general market, the first since the war, opened at the cattle market. Thousands of people turned up to browse through the 350 stalls.

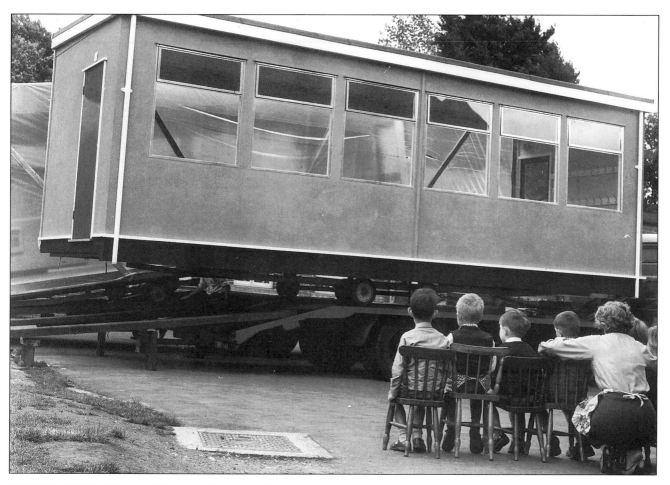

1965 June: Mobile classrooms were such a novelty that the unloading of one at Bridge School provided a spectacle for the pupils. It was the first of its type to be provided for a school in the Canterbury area.

1967 March: Coats with stand-up collars, striped sleeves, tent dresses and the use of man-made fibres such as tricel and crimplene were some of the fashions modelled at Ricemans.

1965 October: Some of the first 460 undergraduates arrive to occupy Eliot College at the University. Rutherford College opened a year later, followed by Keynes in 1968 and Darwin in 1970.

1968 January: A Panda car rendezvous with a police foot patrol in the Precincts during a test run for the new cars, which were about to become fully operational in Canterbury.

1957 May: Telephone House, Canterbury. On the left, reported the *Kentish Gazette*, is the electronic multiplying punch — a version of the so-called electronic brain — and on the right the tabulator which processes the accounts.

1959 April: The first electric train to run in East Kent returns to Canterbury East station after a trial trip to Selling. The full service began in June. Note the spire of St Andrew's Presbyterian Church (since demolished) in the background.

Protest

1964: A coffin and a wrecked car were included in a protest procession through the streets of Bridge on Easter Sunday as part of the villagers' bypass campaign. Eight people had died and 50 had been injured in the village in the previous five years. Bridge bypass opened in June 1976.

1964 October: Women living in Edward Road use dustbins to stop students from the Technical College parking outside their homes. Since the college had opened the previous month the residents of Edward Road and Albert Road had signed a petition asking for parking restrictions to be imposed.

1969 August: Boughton villagers forced A2 traffic to make a 12-mile detour via the Thanet Way when they had a sit-down protest in the main street over road safety fears and a call for a bypass. Boughton bypass opened in March 1976.

1965 June: 300 supporters of the Christian Group of CND, 'pilgrims for peace', complete their walk from Southwark to Canterbury.

1953: A miners' May Day rally outside the old Marlowe Theatre in St Margaret's Street. Next to it is the Freemasons Tavern.

1970 July: Thousands of pilgrims in the Precincts of the Cathedral watched police grapple with two militant Protestants who rushed the altar during a Roman Catholic mass. The mass was the first to be celebrated in the Precincts for 400 years and was held as part of the Cathedral's programme to commemorate the 800th anniversary of the murder of Thomas Becket.

1970 July: The Rev Ian Paisley, Protestant Union MP for North Antrim, was in the city at the time of the Roman Catholic mass but staged his own peaceful demonstration outside the Precincts in the Buttermarket.

1960 September: Residents protest about flies and smells at the city rubbish dump at Tennyson Avenue. Their placards were aimed at councillors making an official inspection of the tip. Note the prefabs in the background.

1967 February: Shifts of up to eight hours long were arranged by University students taking part in their continuous 100-hour vigil in the Buttermarket in protest against American action in Vietnam.

1966 November: University students demonstrate outside Canterbury Sessions House, where Radio 390 (broadcasting from the wartime Red Sands Towers in the Thames Estuary) was the first pirate radio station to be prosecuted. The managing director was Ted Allbeury, later to become a best-selling thriller writer. The company was fined £100 for operating in territorial waters. Four hours after the magistrates' decision the radio station went off the air — but it resumed the following month, claiming new evidence nullified prosecution claims that Red Sands was within the three-mile limit.

Army Life

1952 May: King Frederik IX of Denmark, Colonel-in-Chief of The Buffs, inspects a Guard of Honour at the Barracks at St Martin's Hill. He was in Canterbury to unveil a memorial window in the Warriors' Chapel of the Cathedral to commemorate those soldiers who died in the war.

1953 December: 'Food is 100 per cent better' say the troops who use the new dining hall and kitchen at the Depot, The Buffs. The barracks on St Martin's Hill were built in 1939 as a new depot for The Buffs, who were then in the Old Infantry Barracks in Military Road. War prevented an immediate move but they reopened as The Buffs Depot in 1948. They were renamed Howe Barracks in 1956 in honour of Lieut-Col G.Howe, who commanded the Depot before and during the war. The Home Counties Brigade Depot moved in during 1960.

1960 June: King Frederik IX of Denmark presents new colours to the 4th and 5th Battalions The Buffs at the St Lawrence Ground, watched by 3,000 guests.

1962 November: Brigade Colonel M.Jennings bids farewell to L/Cpl John Jarrett (right), of Upstreet, and the other last National Servicemen to leave the Home Counties Brigade Depot in Canterbury. The three men arrived at Wemyss Barracks on 16 November 1960 — just one day before the end of National Service was announced by the Government. "It was not terribly good for morale," said Col Jennings.

1966 December: The flags of four famous regiments were lowered for the last time at Howe Barracks. With them came down the flag of the Home Counties Brigade Depot. The ceremony marked the passing of four Home Counties regiments: The Queen's Royal Surrey, Queen's Own Buffs (The Royal Kent Regiment), Royal Sussex and Middlesex. Seconds later a fanfare sounded and a new flag was raised, marking the birth of The Queen's Regiment.

1967 December: Disinfected straw was put down at the entrance to Howe Barracks in the fight against the spread of foot and mouth disease.

1948 January: Field-Marshal Viscount Montgomery — who had been given the Freedom of Canterbury in October 1945 — returned to the city during a two-day tour of Kent military establishments. Here, 'Monty' greets Major Tom Burt at the Drill Hall (later the Westgate Hall).

1966 June: Queen Juliana of the Netherlands visited Howe Barracks to inspect the First Battalion, The Royal Sussex Regiment, of which she was Colonel-in-Chief. Those on parade included members of the Regiment's Old Comrades Association.

1957 August: Rides in a carrier were popular at The Buffs' open day at Howe Barracks.

From the Air

St George's Place runs from left to right across the foreground of this pre-war picture, which also shows the old Kent and Canterbury Hospital in Longport. The terrace on the north side suffered in the Blitz.

Dane John dominates this pre-war view. Buildings on Wincheap Green (left) fell victim to the ring road. The roof at Canterbury East railway station, which also covered the tracks, disappeared early in the 1950s.

The Westgate is at the centre of this pre-war view, which also shows (top) Mount's greenhouses on Forty Acres Road, now developed for housing in the Pine Tree Avenue area.

A train (top right) puffs its way out of Canterbury West station on the old Canterbury to Whitstable line in this aerial view before the war.

Looking from the Westgate (bottom left) towards St Martin's Hill (right) and beyond, with the Cathedral dominating the centre of this pre-war picture.

Looking down on the then new East Kent Road Car Company garage (centre) in St Stephen's Road before the war. Canterbury West goods yard is in the foreground; on the right, at the junction of The Causeway, is Westgate Mill; the playing field is Blore's Piece, owned by the King's School.

Canterbury Prison and St Martin's Church are near neighbours in this pre-war view. The North Holmes Road and Christ Church College areas have yet to be developed.

The old Kent and Canterbury Hospital in Longport and St Augustine's Abbey ruins take centre stage in this view before the war. Closer to the foreground (in Lower Chantry Lane) is the Payne-Smith School, which was destroyed in the Blitz.

This post-war aerial view shows the cleared blitzed area within the city walls before rebuilding began.

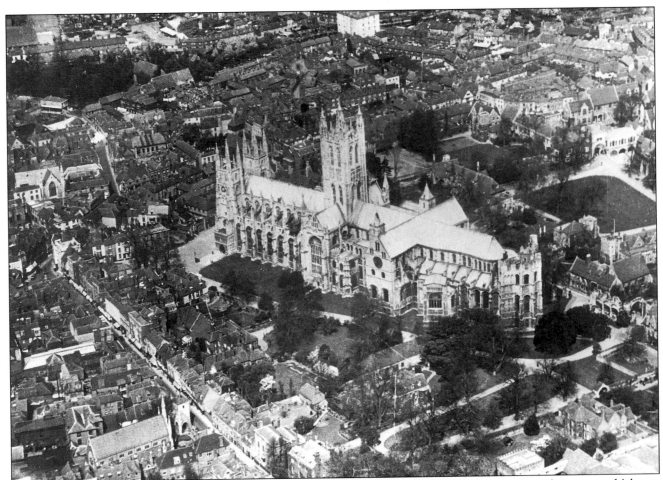

Just visible (bottom right) is the crenellated tower of the Star Brewery, in Broad Street at the junction with Burgate, which was demolished in 1930. Burgate itself runs diagonally across the left of the picture; to the right is the Green Court of King's School.

The old outdoor swimming baths off Whitehall Road were built by the side of the Stour in 1876 (in the Toddlers Cove area) and measured 375ft by 75ft. Swimming was banned on health grounds during the war and the pool was later used for boating. As late as 1966 the council was still hoping to reopen the baths, despite its plans for the £277,000 pool at Kingsmead, which opened in 1970. The Rheims Way of the early 1960s was to come between Victoria recreation ground (top left) and the houses at the end of Queen's Avenue (towards the top right).

Outside the Walls

1930s: Looking down St Dunstan's towards the Westgate, with the level crossing gates closed. Some of the buildings on the left in this view (possibly from 1939) were destroyed in the Blitz — including the taller building, which stood on the corner of Station Road West.

Hales Place, St Stephen's. The original mansion, built in the 1760s, is just left of centre. The estate was sold by Mary Hales to French Jesuits, who established a college there about 1880. They extended the building with two wings and a new block and the college became known as St Mary's. After the Jesuits left in 1928 the building fell into disrepair and was eventually demolished — and the estate was developed for housing in the 1950s. *Picture: Paul Crampton.*

1957 January: The Hales Place estate takes shape. The old drive to the mansion became Hales Drive.

1961 January: High Street (St Gregory's) — looking towards Artillery Street from Northgate. Redevelopment in the 1960s would change this area dramatically.

1959 September: Another landmark going. The hop oast in Dover Street, built in 1811, shortly before it was demolished.

1964 October: The new road between St Stephen's and Whitstable Road was a continuation of the former Forty Acres Road/Beaconsfield Road cul-de-sac — and some questioned whether this narrow road was wide enough to cope with traffic surging through the wider approach.

1963 January: The technical college takes shape despite the heavy snow that winter.

1963 July: Christ Church College being built off North Holmes Road, as seen from the top of St Augustine's gateway.

1937: The Kent and Canterbury Hospital the year it opened, replacing the old hospital in Longport.

1945 July: The first 'temporary house of the American bungalow type' (better known as prefabs) made its appearance in Canterbury at Vauxhall Avenue.

1957 August: Strolling amid the ruins of St Augustine's Abbey.

1956 October: The four-storey Barton Mill straddles the Stour off Sturry Road. There is little to show that a few years before, in August 1951, a serious fire badly damaged about a third of it.

Looking down a narrow, winding Whitehall Bridge Road before the post-war development of the area for housing. This view possibly dates from the 1940s.

1941: Looking down Lower Chantry Lane towards Longport. Two rows of cottages and the Payne-Smith School in this area were destroyed in the war.

A similar view along Lower Chantry Lane some years later. By the time this picture was taken the sites had been cleared and grass and weeds had taken a firm hold.

1965 June: The University, which opened a few months later, continues to take shape. Eliot College was the first to take students. Rutherford, Keynes and Darwin Colleges opened in 1966, 1968 and 1970 respectively.

1962 October: The reasonably dry summer had put the building of the Rheims Way ahead of schedule. London Road veers

...ft in this view from the Harbledown end.

1954 spring: The *Kentish Gazette* moved from a blitzed site in St George's Street to its new building in St George's Place. The offices — which now have another storey — were described as a 'bold contemporary design'.

1964 Spring: Church Lane, St Radigund's. The building on the left is now the site of a sunken garden along part of the old city wall.

1966 October: The Whitehall Baths in flood. The city council was still hoping to re-open them for swimmers, despite plans for the £277,000 pool at Kingsmead, which opened in 1970.

1953 January: The access road to the new cattle market being built at St Stephen's. On the right is what remains of a bungalow demolished to make way for it.

1930s: This terrace stood on the north side of St George's Place until it was destroyed by fire in the Blitz. The house with the wisteria, the home of Dr Wacher, is now the site of the *Kentish Gazette* offices.

Subscribers

Peter Aurup
Audrey Benton-Mayatt
John R. Bliss
Keith Bolton
John R. Brent
Mr J. Frank Brockbank
Joan M. Chapman
Revd Marjorie A. Cobb
Albert Charles Cocks
M.E. Cornish JP
Susan Crowley
Paddy & Mary Currid
Bryan Dachtler
S. Dunford
Barry Everett
Mr Alan G. Finch
Elizabeth Harrison
Mavis L. Holder
A.R. Hopper
Wendy Jane Hyland
Raymond Thomas Kelk
Mark Kemp
Mary Kemsley-Beautridge
Les & Brenda
Irene & Victor Lewis
Miss D.G.S. Lloyd
Mr F. Ludlam
John E.M. Martin
Leonie J. Martin
H.C. Masters
David Matthews
Mrs L. Mirfin
R.H. & S.M. Morgan

Eric James Morris
John Nunn
William A. Oakey
Nigel Outred
Kathleen Parker
Jean Pegg
David Penny
Idina M. Plummer
Marilyn Potts
Margaret Rennie
Mr Charles F. Robinson
K.J. Ross
Miss P.A. Smith
J.E. Spanner
N.B. Spary
Peter Stannard
Anita Steere
Miss M. Sweetingham
Mrs B.H. Taylor
Eileen M. Terry
Nigel J. Tilly
Bill Trickett
Ken Turner
Nigel Uden
Ernest Walker
Malcolm F. Walkinshaw
Bob Wanstall
John Wehner
Leonard Austin Hayward Welch
Mrs S.M. White
Mrs E. Wilkinson
David Woodward
M.M. Young